You Don't Always
Get What You Ask For

Lessons of Love from Dad

Jim Wilcox

Beacon Hill Press of Kansas City
Kansas City, Missouri

Copyright 2001
by Beacon Hill Press of Kansas City

ISBN 083-411-8939

Printed in the
United States of America

Cover Design: Ted Ferguson

Library of Congress Cataloging-in-Publication Data

Wilcox, Jim.
    You don't always get what you ask for : lessons of love from Dad / Jim Wilcox.
        p. cm.
    ISBN 0-8341-1893-9 (pbk.)
        1. Fathers—Religious life. 2. Fatherhood—Religious aspects—Christianity.
    3. Wilcox, Jim. I. Title: You do not always get what you ask for. II. Title.

    BV4529.17 .W555 2001
    248.8'421—dc21

                                                                00-065187

10 9 8 7 6 5 4 3 2 1

To
Ben and Josh—
there are simply
no better young men.

Dad's Daily Devotional

I asked my Father for an ounce of grace;
    He walked in torment to the Cross.

I asked my Father for a measure of mercy;
    He took me to the Sea of Forgetfulness.

I asked my Father for just a little justice;
    He handed me the Golden Rule.

I asked my Father for a sense of profound peace;
    He led me beside quiet waters.

I asked my Father for a whit of wisdom;
    He told me to follow His footprints.

I asked my Father for a pittance of patience;
    He opened my mind to toleration.

I asked my Father for a course of action;
    He provided the rock for my foundation.

Contents

1

Grace

I asked my Father for an ounce of grace;
He walked in torment to the Cross.

It comes in the mail probably twice a week—more often during holiday seasons. It comes on the front of magazines, on large envelopes with plastic windows, attached to samples of cereal or detergent, and atop credit card enticements by the dozens.

And it has easily become my pet peeve of word abuse. As an English teacher, I study words and phrases pretty much all the time, and I'm now at the age when I have a long list of "pet peeves"—things like "round circle," "tiny infant," "actual fact," "completely destroyed," "very hot fire," or "slightly pregnant."

But the one that gets to me the most is the promise for a "FREE GIFT." Now let me ask you something, have you ever received a gift that wasn't free to you?

If the answer is yes, then I'm sorry to be the one to tell you that you didn't get a gift. What you got was an obligation. If the answer is no, then I must ask you why some yahoo thought it necessary to use the modifier *free*.

That's like the student of mine who once told me that for graduation she received "$300 worth of money." Or the student who wrote that "people often die because of health reasons." Or the freshman who wrote that "when experimenting with an animal in a microwave, the animal often explodes, *and this can be painful*."

Exploding painful? Nah! And why was anyone putting an animal in a microwave, anyway? What, exactly, was the experiment?

I've actually edited manuscripts that have included sentences like "It is our choice to choose" and "The last resort to punish rapists is decapitation, but that is such a permanent solution" and "A smoker is twice as likely to die as a nonsmoker" and "The Kirby vacuum cleaner is great for cleaning your cracks and crevices."

You stay away from me with that vacuum, Boy!

To be honest (and why wouldn't I be?), these bloopers, as I call them, are one of the primary reasons I keep teaching. They're gifts to me on those long Oklahoma afternoons when I wonder if I can read one more freshman essay about a high school relationship that ended in utter despair.

One of the best gifts I ever received was a bicycle about 10 years ago. My wife had been promising me (a.k.a. *herself*) a new garage door opener for months so *I* wouldn't have to get out in the rain anymore to open the garage door for *her*.

So that Christmas Eve I wasn't all that surprised to open a small box with a garage door remote control inside. Not surprised, but hugely disappointed. I pictured myself all of Christmas break trying to install some contraption (emphasis on "trap") while dreaming of pedaling all around the state in subfreezing temperatures on a new mountain bike, which is all I had asked for that Christmas.

"Go outside and hit the button," she told me, to the sheer delight of our two little boys.

"What on earth for?" I asked. "It's like 15 degrees out there!" But I acquiesced and threw on a windbreaker.

Nothing happened the first few punches, but eventually the garage door at our next door neighbor's house began to ascend. "Uh-oh," I thought. "Now I've done it. What if I've deactivated his pacemaker too?"

Then I saw it. Black. Twenty-six inches high. Twelve speeds. Sitting all alone in the middle of my neighbor's nearly empty garage. A shiny new mountain bike. I couldn't remember when I'd been that happy.

I will always remember, on the other hand, the Christmas my twin brother gave me a beautiful sweater. He had graduated from college and immediately found a teaching job, whereas I had graduated from college and headed off to seminary to fall deeper into debt.

As my trip home neared, I racked my brain to think about what I might buy for my family that wouldn't prevent me from eating the next month. For John, I bought some new underwear and threw into the package a slightly worn silk tie. (As it turned out, he was quite grateful I hadn't given him a new tie and *slightly worn underwear.*)

I felt so small Christmas morning when he opened my tiny gift and I opened his lavish present to me. He was gracious, but I learned that day that even if I had to eat cheese the entire month of January, he would never outgive me again.

He has made that promise very hard to keep because he still makes more money than I do, and he loves to spend it.

Max Lucado wrote a book a few years ago, titled *In the Grip of Grace*. I started to read it back then but could never get past chapter 4 because it affected me so deeply. I've been trying to process it ever since.

In that passage, he writes about serial killer and cannibal Jeffrey Dahmer, the young man who, over a period of a couple of years, seduced, raped, murdered, and subsequently consumed parts of 17 boys in an American suburb.

Lucado states that as heinous as those crimes were, that's not what bothers him about Jeffrey Dahmer. And as hideous as that deviant mind must have been, that's not what bothers him about Jeffrey Dahmer, either. And as gruesome as that trial must have been for the victims' families, that's not what bothers him about Jeffrey Dahmer, either.

No, what bothers Max Lucado most about Jeffrey Dahmer is that one day he will see the human cannibal in heaven. According to the most reliable sources, before he, himself, was murdered in prison, Dahmer had found the cross of Jesus was for him, too, and was leading Bible studies up to the day he was killed.

Lucado writes that a *grace* that is that free, a *grace* that will reach down that far and change the life of a society's worst nightmare is a *gift* that is completely incomprehensible. It is a *gift* that is beyond human understanding.

What Jesus did on Calvary did not simply cover "misdemeanors" or little "white lies" or "sins of thought." Jesus did not shed His messianic blood to make us feel better about ourselves or to allow us to register Republican or to fill a bunch of Christian churches every Sunday morning.

Jesus died for Jeffrey Dahmer and those like him. Like us. Jesus came to be Light in the darkness—the deepest, blackest, inkiest, foulest, most hellish darkness there is.

Praise His name!

If that doesn't change the way you think about the grace, graciousness, and gracefulness of fatherhood, nothing will.

> *Amazing grace! how sweet the sound!*
> *That saved a wretch like me!*
> I *once was lost, but now am found;*
> *Was blind, but now I see.*

2

Mercy

I asked my Father for a measure of mercy;
He took me to the Sea of Forgetfulness.

The day I became a father, I knew how much God loved me.

Up to that point, all I knew was what the Bible and its preachers had told me about how much my Heavenly Father loved me. It was theoretical, not practical. It was hearsay, not comprehensible truth. It was a matter of faith, not yet of experience.

But when I wrapped my long arms around that tiny, squirming bundle of promise and potential for the first time in Mercy Medical Center (I'm not making that up), I felt such overwhelming devotion, affection, and tenderness that I understood in a powerful way how Jesus Christ felt when He went to the Cross for *me*.

How any father can encounter that moment without having that same spiritual epiphany is sincerely beyond me. There is literally no distance I

wouldn't travel, no sacrifice I wouldn't suffer, no tur-
moil I wouldn't endure for either of my sons. None.
The moment they were born, their happiness and
contentment superseded my own. That's a "father
thing," I think.

That is not to say, of course, that I became completely selfless and would on any given day be mis-
taken for Mother Teresa. Not even close. But that
passage into parenthood on June 19, 1980, then
again on April 26, 1983, did change me profoundly:
I began a journey that evening toward the enlighten-
ment of mercy that has given me a prophetic glimpse
of the Godhead.

What every father must recognize immediately is
that he is not a mother. (I don't suppose you realized
that until now, did you?) Upon that recognition,
what every father needs to do is try to emulate the
mother of his children. That's how I have learned to
be a decent parent—attempting to follow my wife's
footprints of compassion and mercy, watching her be
the best mother in the universe. Despite her multiple
talents, when it comes to her sons, this woman is ut-
terly selfless.

It's that "mother thing," and she's got a terminal
case of it.

A few years ago, I wrote a tribute to her and my
own mother, titled "When," which I gave to them on
Mother's Day.

When your mom told you it would hurt her more than it would hurt you, she was telling you the truth.

When your mom told you "because I said so," what she meant was that you were a generation away from understanding why.

When your mom told you to eat your vegetables, what she meant was that she wanted you to be strong and healthy more than she wanted you to like her.

When your mom told you to clean up your room before you played outside, what she meant was that for every privilege to enjoy in life, there is a responsibility to honor.

When your mom told you to be home by 11:00, what she meant was that a big part of her heart would be missing until you brought it back to her.

When your mom snuggled up to your dad or held his hand on long walks, what she wanted you to see was that being in love is the greatest gift you'll ever have on earth.

When your mom knelt by her bed at night to pray, what she was admitting was that loving you was a job so big it took both her and God to do it right.

And after you fell asleep each night when you were little, what you never knew was that your mom sat next to your bed in the dark, gazing at her baby.

And dreaming sweet dreams.

Long ago, I confessed to myself that I am the chief of sinners, and if God can forgive me, then obviously He has enough mercy to go around. It's been quite liberating, actually, to recognize my appropriate place as "low man on the totem pole" at home, work, and church. That may sound crazy, but then, much of the gospel is pretty "crazy," isn't it?

As a result of that admission, saying "I'm sorry" to anyone I might have offended or crossed has become no big deal. (Of course, it helps that 99 percent of the people I've said it to have been quite forgiving.)

That includes my kids. If there is anyone in the world easy to offend, it's a parent's kids—especially when they become teenagers. One of my favorite things to do before they could drive themselves to school was to drop them off right in front of the main entrance, where all the "cool kids" had gathered to giggle, and as I drove off, roll down the window and shout loud enough to wake the dead, "I LOVE YOU." Sometimes in a falsetto. Sometimes honking all the way down the road.

I've learned to be sorry for that embarrassment, but at the time it was so much fun.

When our older son got old enough to go out on his own, he made some decisions his mother and I did not like. For a while, he tried smoking cigarettes because he wanted to fit in with the group he was hanging around. It killed me. (Somehow, his mom knew it wouldn't last, but being the worrywart I am, I pictured myself having to arrange for his funeral.)

One afternoon, Ben and I were home alone, and I *had* to talk to him again. After initially denying it, he told me he was smoking again, but "not much." I gave him my Reader's Digest version of what could happen to his body if he continued, then I just broke down.

"Ben, you're slowly killing yourself, and that means you're killing a part of me. You're killing a part of your brother. And you are absolutely killing a big part of your mother."

He suddenly changed his attitude and tone. He began to realize that his actions affected more than himself. He was hurting his family.

I kept laying on the guilt trip. "What if your brother sees his big brother, whom he looks up to, smoking and slowly killing himself, and then he begins smoking too. Can you handle that?"

"No," he said and began to think hard. He told me he was sorry and that he would quit. We hugged for a long time, and I told him I forgave him.

And even if he slips up again in the future, I will forgive him. Because he's my son and I just can't help it.

Just like God can't help it with me. And you.

3

Justice

I asked my Father for just a little justice;
He handed me the Golden Rule.

Short of a real judge in a black robe beginning a statement with, "Therefore, I hereby sentence you to . . . ," few sentences in the English language carry as much fear and dread for a child as Mom's exasperated admonition: "You just wait until your father gets home!"

(At my house, it is always the other way around: "You just wait until your mother gets home!" I'd say as I flipped the channel over to *Judge Judy.*)

Christian parenting walks a tightrope between two seemingly contrasting mandates: the proverb, "Spare the rod, spoil the child," and the Golden Rule, "Do unto others as you would have them do unto you."

The former sounds at first like divine instruction to beat the tar out of our children with a nine iron anytime they spill their milk or break a house rule. (Nothing could be farther from its meaning.) The latter limits our responses to such situations by asking us to inflict only that amount of suffering we, ourselves, would want. (And few of us want to suffer anything at all, ever.)

The secret to effective parenting lies somewhere in between.

In Old Testament times, the shepherd's rod was used sparingly as a tool of punishment; after all, what good is it to beat the bleat out of an animal as stupid as a sheep?

Typically, the rod was a guide to the herd, steering them to nourishment, shelter, or safety. Occasionally, it would be used to rescue a sheep that might have fallen into a crevice or gotten wedged between two bushes or trees.

So Solomon was never advocating corporal punishment when he alluded to imagery available in his day; instead, he seems to be advising us as parents to actively guide our children toward spiritual, psychological, and physical nourishment, shelter, and safety.

There are literally hundreds of books on the market about how to raise a child correctly. Sometimes it seems that anyone who has ever given birth to a baby or sired an infant has proclaimed himself or herself an "expert" in bringing up Junior. For every book that advises spanking a child as the only effective form of punishment, there are three books that advise against it. Some even teach a combination of physical punishment for some "crimes" and other "creative" punishment of other "crimes."

Usually, most parents succumb to using whatever punishment was doled out on them when they were youngsters trying to survive. (Tragically, this explains why child abuse is often cyclical: the abused often grow up to become abusers.)

If you were put in a time-out chair, chances are high that you use that method with your children. If you were grounded, you probably employ that technique. And if you were spanked, you undoubtedly know where all the paddles are in your house today.

God's grace has allowed me to forget all but two spankings I received as a mischievous identical twin of a mischievous instigator. (If he wants to blame me, he can write his own book.)

The first took place late on a Saturday morning. Earlier, my brother and his friend, Doug Brunner, had smeared a "canine lawn ornament" on our next door neighbor's tricycle seat; when Mikey jumped onto his trusty steed, his stinky bottom nearly slipped all the way off, probably causing minor discomfort.

The bigger pain was to his ego as John, Doug, and I were watching and found great humor in Mikey's slippage and stinkage. It wasn't until Mikey ran, screaming, into his house and fetched his mother that John and Doug realized their grave predicament.

They ran away, whereupon Mikey's mom went

and got my dad, who jumped into the family car to retrieve the fugitives, who couldn't have gone far because we were not allowed to cross the street, and not even Doug could convince my brother to break that law.

Once returned, Doug was sent home and John and I were escorted into our room, where my dad, an elementary school principal who had taken courses in paddling malcontents, told my brother to "drop trow" and grab his ankles. Several swats brought forth the desired effect.

Thinking I had escaped such punishment because I had been only an observer and not a participant, I had another think coming. I got punished in like manner for not exercising the judgment to turn in my brother and friend before the act took place.

What I learned that day is that doing whatever it takes to stop a crime is far less painful than the humiliation of being dubbed the "Neighborhood Nark." I'm not sure what my brother learned.

The last spanking I remember ever getting was at the hand (literally) of my mom, whose favorite preamble seemed to be, "This is gonna hurt me a lot more than it's gonna hurt you." I never understood that . . . until I became a father.

Unfortunately for Mom, this warning of hers was a bad omen. After she left the room where John and I were pretending to cry, she went out to the living room and watched in horror as her spanker's hand began to swell and turn purple. Then blue. Apparently, she had broken several blood vessels in her hand while administering justice and would suffer for a couple of days hence.

As a dad, I reserved spanking for defiant disobedience or endangerment, which meant I spanked my boys maybe a half-dozen times in their youth. The last time I spanked either one of them was the night I put the younger one to bed after giving him a swat earlier in the evening for something dreadful, I'm sure.

While changing him into his pajamas, I noticed my red handprint on his precious bottom and wept just as much as he had earlier. I vowed at that moment never to strike my little boy again.

What I have learned—both as a son and as a father—and as a Christian citizen is the truth and *wisdom* of Jesus' "Golden Rule." Paraphrased, it tells me that "To be like Christ, I should treat every person with whom I come into contact as if he or she were Christ."

Would I strike another human being if I imagined him or her to be Jesus? Would I cry out for "justice" in the name of "capital punishment" if I envisioned Jesus strapped down to that gurney? Would I gossip about another if he or she were Christ? Would I neglect someone if he or she were Jesus? Would I condemn in judgment someone if he or she were Jesus?

These are difficult questions, indeed.

But if we believe not only the words of Christ but also His life, then we must answer the tough questions with equally perplexing responses and actions. Jesus gave His life in the place of a murderer, Barabbas, and thereby gave His life for my sins. And yours.

When it comes to the Son of God, not only did He tell us to "Do unto others as you would have them do unto you," but He actually *did* it!

4

Peace

I asked my Father for a sense of profound peace;
He led me beside quiet waters.

If the antonym of "peace like a river" is "stress like a stormy sea," then I spent most of my life on a life raft atop 30-foot swells. In the past, there just never seemed to be enough time, resources, or energy to finish the tasks at hand in the way I felt was necessary to call myself a success, and my health began to pay a high price.

In college, I was treated for ulcers that turned out to be nothing more than a stressed-out semester. Years later, I found myself so emotionally spent trying to do two full-time jobs at the same time that I was literally wailing at the walls that seemed to be closing in around me.

Just a few years ago, doctors began treating me for high blood pressure then testing me for cancer, both eventually downgraded to symptoms of stress. Even when I thought I was having a heart attack after a claustrophobic banquet four years ago, I discovered I was experiencing what they call a panic attack.

Since then, I have sought counseling and through therapy have discovered that life doesn't have to be a series of crises; rather, it can, and indeed has, become a series of celebrations.

I have discovered what the hymnist intended when he wrote, "When peace like a river attendeth my way, / When sorrows like sea billows roll, / Whatever my lot, Thou hast taught me to say, / 'It is well, it is well with my soul.'"

When I was a little boy, my parents found a "heaven on earth" officially named Camp Fresno, though it was more appropriately called Dinkey Creek by those who visited every year. Nestled in the Sierra Nevada Mountains of central California, this haven of rest became for me the idyllic picture of what heaven will be like.

Our cabin was a simple two-room abode: a kitchen with a cast-iron wood stove, and a room with two sets of bunk beds and a double bed. It didn't matter that spider webs graced every corner or wasps went in and out the open-air windows at will because we were in the mountains and every day provided enough adventure to fill a dozen Tom Sawyer books.

The blue jays joined the symphony of scents every morning as coffee, bacon, and recently chopped wood awoke us to witness the sun urging its way through the surrounding forest. We spent our mornings playing campsite volleyball with others and our afternoons hiking the shady paths or "swimming" in the ice-cold creek.

Perhaps my fondest memory is catching my first fish—a massive 6-inch rainbow trout—and preparing it for dinner that evening. Only a child's imagination could recall it feeding a family of five until they could eat no more.

Now I'm not necessarily an advocate of transcendental meditation, but more than once I have conjured up those placid days at Dinkey Creek to calm my anxious spirit during times of undue stress. I truly believe the Holy Spirit gave me those childhood memories in order to "lead me beside quiet waters" and "restore my soul."

The truth to finding peace is learning to look at life through a telescope, not a microscope. To analyze every sordid detail of every sorry event as if that will help anything is really a waste of the human spirit. Believe me—I know of what I speak. I have lain awake too many nights of my life, imagining how I might have done something differently in order to solve a dilemma or ease an emergency.

Reliving and living are not the same thing. And preliving is not the same as living, either.

How many times have you been so afraid of the future, so worried about what might or might not happen tomorrow or next week or next year that you have become immobilized? How healthy is that? How many of those fears and worries have actually occurred?

If you're like most of us, about 90 percent of what we worry about never takes place . . . and the other 10 percent seems to take care of itself.

For example, I used to worry about plumbing problems *all the time*. I'm not kidding—ALL THE TIME. Every time I saw a repair truck roaming through the neighborhood, I just knew he was headed for the flood that was happening somewhere in my house.

I attribute this phobia to one of two traumas in my life. When I was a little boy, I was riding on my tricycle one morning and looked back at a playmate at precisely the wrong moment. When I turned back around, I ran face-first into the back of a plumber's truck, pipes creasing my baby fat in perfect circles. I bore round scabs for days.

The other experience happened after I became a homeowner. One Saturday morning, my wife and I passed each other in the kitchen before the kids got up. Still only semiconscious, she said the fatal words, "Do you think you could fix the leaky faucet in my bathroom?"

I just kept on walking into the garage and got my hammer. And a Phillips screwdriver. I figured one of those tools had to work. I began to unscrew the knobs and when I got to the last thread on the "hot" side, the screw shot, and I mean *shot*, toward the ceiling like a .22-caliber bullet, just narrowly missing my eye.

That produced a geyser of steaming hot water that began to eat a hole in the ceiling, so I threw the trash out of the can and into the hallway, all over my wife (accidentally), and inverted it over Old Faithful (the geyser, not my wife).

"Hold this," I screamed. "I'll get Steve."

Steve was my next-door neighbor who looked like someone who would know what to do, in that he was very large. I threw on some shorts and dashed to get him.

The first thing he did when he got to my bathroom was look at my wife, who was still in her nightgown, holding a trash can over a spewing faucet hole. Then he jumped under the sink to look for the shutoff valve. I had already done that, but I thought he might actually find one. He didn't.

"I'll run out and shut off the main in the front yard," he shouted.

Dodging our sons who were now in the hallway in only their underwear, he ran for the front door. Then he ran *through* the front door. My wife had cleaned the storm door so thoroughly, Steve didn't even see it and suddenly he was sprawled across the front porch with shards of glass all around and over him, including in his face and hands.

29

Our seven-year-old knew what was happening. He ran into the living room and with the look of a deer caught in headlights began screaming, "TORNADO! TORNADO! TORNADO!" For little Ben, the End was nigh, and he was gonna get caught in his Fruit of the Looms.

Once the water was shut off, things calmed down tremendously, but it was not until that evening that everything had returned to normal with a new storm door, a new bathroom ceiling, and a new 5-cent rubber washer on the bathroom hot water faucet.

Ever since then, I have hated all drips and all plumbing trucks.

Yet I have learned that plumbing fiascos happen to everyone sometime or another. And smoking electrical outlets are fixable. And dead car batteries can be recharged. And if life didn't have all of these little adventures, a lot of people would be out of jobs and forced to teach college writing courses.

Then I'd be out of a job and really have something to worry about. To be honest, it is these plumbing adventures that have made the phrase "quiet waters" so meaningful to me. And that's another reason Dinkey Creek has meant so much to me: no indoor plumbing.

Ah, that will be heaven to me.

5

Wisdom

I asked my Father for a whit of wisdom;
He told me to follow His footprints.

One of the hardest scriptural pills to swallow is prescribed by Dr. James at the beginning of his letter to the Church: "Consider it pure joy, my brothers, whenever you face trials of many kinds, because you know that the testing of your faith develops perseverance. Perseverance must finish its work so that you may be mature and complete, not lacking anything. If any of you lacks wisdom, he should ask God, who gives generously to all without finding fault, and it will be given to him" (James 1:2-5). I've been through a few trials (and tribulations, according to the King James Version), and, frankly, if they were anything at the time, "pure joy" wasn't the first thing that came to mind. Not even close.

One of the most difficult trials I have faced in my life was the desertion of the young woman I loved just a month before we were supposed to get married. She had flown home for a week to "work on wedding plans" but came back a month later to pack up and leave.

No reasons. No excuses. No warnings. And no wedding.

For weeks, I roamed the woods behind the seminary I was attending, contemplating suicide, certain not only of her defection but of God's too. Surely a God who loved me as much as He said He did would never have left me all alone at the altar of matrimony, sucking for air as if the atmosphere had suddenly become a complete vacuum.

As trite as it may sound, He didn't leave me alone. As a matter of testimony, as soon as *she* left me, He sent His angels to surround my crumbled and crushed spirit. Two angel-friends kept me from doing anything "stupid" to myself until I began to breathe evenly again months later.

After a year of mourning and grieving the relationship I had once thought would last forever, I was introduced to a young lady who not only gave me hope but showed me a love I had never seen. Although I was scared to death of committing that much of myself to another person ever again, I learned through time and the building of trust that life before Linda no longer mattered.

Did I feel "pure joy" in the middle of my self-destruction? Was I happy about developing perseverance so that I could be "mature and complete, not lacking in anything"?

You're kidding, right?

Did I feel "pure joy" when Linda told me in front of family and friends two years later that she would love me forever, no matter how much hair I lost or how much weight I gained, how little money I might make or how much time I would spend with sports?

"Pure joy" doesn't even come close.

Do I feel "pure joy" years later, now that I'm involved in a ministry that brings me into contact with young people who are frequently at the end of their lifelines, desperate for a word of advice or a bit of wisdom that will rescue their hearts? Praise the Lord, I do. I do. I do. After all, I was being prepared for such a ministry that terrible autumn 25 years ago when I, myself, was as desperate as people get. I am living proof to hundreds of college students today that one can and *will* survive some of life's worst blows. I am living proof that God is faithful.

Not only that, but as a father, I have found that just about every trial I persevered as a child and young person has allowed me the credibility my two sons are searching for as they mature into young men. Because I have "been there," they can trust me.

For the past several years, people all over the country have started sporting canvas bracelets on their wrists with the four letters "WWJD." I've even seen several stars in the NBA wearing them during televised games. The Christian bookstore just down the street has a complete line of WWJD jewelry in gold, sterling silver, and pewter. Three or four kiosks full of the stuff.

(My cynical question always is, "Would Jesus Wear That?")

The bottom line, however, is that nothing could be wiser than to ask that question before every major decision: what would Jesus do? As dads, were we to ask that before we disciplined our kids, celebrated with them, spent time with or away from them, worked or played or studied with them, we would be magnificently better parents.

And someday, if we're terribly blessed, not only will our kids ask that same question when they become "mature and complete," but they might also ask, "What would Dad do?"

6

Patience

I asked my Father for a pittance of patience;
He opened my mind to toleration.

I was born two weeks premature, and I've been impatient ever since. As an eight-pound twin of an eight-pound twin, my mother was becoming more than a little impatient herself.

"Will you *P-L-E-A-S-E* come outta there?"

My mom's father was born seven *years* premature. His parents wanted to name him after a sitting president, but as staunch Republicans, they weren't about to stick him with the name of the Democrat Grover Cleveland. For seven years, they simply called my grandfather, "Boy" or "Son."

Then in 1901, Grandpa Crawford got his name: William McKinley.

When I pray for patience, therefore, what I'm really praying for is a miracle. I'm so impatient, I sometimes eat dessert first. I'm so impatient, I occasionally read the last page of a novel before I crack the spine. I'm so impatient, I can't bring myself to buy green bananas. I'm so impatient, I actually wrote chapter 7 of this book first. (And this chapter last.)

I wish I were more patient with my two sons, but probably the thing that has allowed me the most patience in raising them is remembering all the stupid stuff I did as a kid.

Like the recess I took a classmate's "show-and-tell" health book out to show my friends the full-body diagrams inside. Mark's selfish yank followed by nature's sudden gust blew some of the pages all over northern California, and let me tell you, Mr. Davis was not pleased.

Or the recess my brother and I tricked several kids into listening to a bogus tale while the other one knelt behind the victim. A quick shove put the dope on the turf, and we all laughed as if we were ready for *The Ed Sullivan Show*.

When we got home with a 31-word sentence to write 50 times as punishment, my brother and I found my parents' stash of carbon paper and expedited the procedure considerably. Unfortunately, we were too stupid to throw the carbons away, and when Mom and Dad found the evidence of our deceit, we suffered retribution far harsher than 1,550 words.

Or the night we were three hours late getting home because the car we were driving—a coral 1963 Rambler Classic 660—was stopped by three police cruisers in a nearby town, guns drawn, bullhorns blaring, threatening to blow us into kingdom come if we didn't cooperate.

Apparently we fit the description of a drug-deal/car-theft ring, and six apparently bored officers took their time to realize the lunacy of suspecting two skinny nerds who had never had a sip of alcohol, much less the wherewithal to deal cocaine, of "stealing" a coral 1963 Rambler Classic 660.

Or the afternoon I tried to save my brother a few minutes of California rush hour traffic by meeting him *on the highway* (literally) for our ride home from our summer jobs. As soon as he saw his only brother *on the highway,* he slammed on his brakes to see why I was *on the highway,* forcing every car behind him to subsequently slam on its brakes.

Unfortunately for both of us, one such vehicle was a highway patrolman who instantly pulled him over and made me join my rather angry brother in the front seat of our 1969 VW Beetle. Imagine the officer's impatience when he looked at our licenses and couldn't tell us apart.

"Now which one of you was *on the highway* and which one of you stopped all traffic from here to Santa Cruz?"

Or the summer we were left alone while Mom and Dad went to Europe, and one day we accidentally left the door of the deep freezer in the garage open. By the time we found it the next morning, the garage floor was full of defrosted frost water mixed with blood from the half a beef they had recently purchased.

Knowing humans could not eat refrozen meat, we were forced to cook it all that day. A half a beef. Several chickens. Some pork chops. We had a neighborhood barbecue in our backyard the likes of which have never been duplicated, feeding some people we had never even met. Sorry to say we did not collect 12 basketsful afterward.

Mom and Dad returned later that month to half a pound of hamburger and a frozen pint of peaches . . . and two rather contrite boys.

Today, when I recall such mistakes and accidents and "I didn't mean to" statements, it's a little bit easier for me to tolerate the fallibility of my own children.

If you sometimes question your own patience, you might want to study this brief checklist. Once you discover your "patience quotient," you may have to decide whether or not you need to write a 31-word sentence 50 times. (I recommend 2 Cor. 1:6.)

You know you are impatient . . .

- when you pick up the TV remote and try to call your office for messages
- when you start thinking of Communion as Sunday dinner's appetizer
- when you sleep in your shoes and socks in order to save a few minutes in the morning

- when you can hardly shave in your car on the way to work because you're trying to dictate the report due yesterday over your mobile phone
- when you honk at cars in front of you even though the light is still red
- when you think a radar detector would be a splendid birthday present
- when you try to fast-forward through the news
- when you drive around a parking lot for 10 minutes in an attempt to find the perfect parking spot
- when your blood pressure is higher than your IQ
- when your primary source of protein is your fingernails

7

Course of Action

I asked my Father for a course of action;
He provided the rock for my foundation.

Television plays a powerful role in our culture, dictating its values and images to anybody with both the time to couch himself or herself and the ability to hold a remote control and aim it. For an average of more than seven hours a day, households are inundated with more information and propaganda than can be processed with any kind of mature discernment.

Both its critics and its champions have produced volumes of studies that have shown TV to be the most influential medium ever created, for good and ill alike. It has been linked to heinous acts of deprivation, particularly among the most vulnerable slice of the populace: children. On the other hand, it has allowed us all to access the heights of human accomplishment, permitting us to dream and hope and imagine discoveries or adventures once thought impossible.

It is no surprise, then, that when children are asked to make a list of their heroes, they include— sometimes exclusively—those icons from the 25" box plugged into the wall. That can be either greatly exciting or terribly frightening, depending on the programs they've seen and, of course, other influences, like family and church and school.

Children who regularly, if not religiously, watch cartoons depicting action heroes who soar through space invariably hope to one day become astronauts with superhuman capabilities. Youngsters who are exposed to 24 hours of sports every day become obsessed with becoming the next Michael Jordan or Wayne Gretzky or Mark McGwire. And kids who are glued to VH-1 or MTV spend their nights dreaming of playing guitars or drums in front of 100,000 screaming fans in Wembley Stadium.

Fortunately, dads have a tremendous power to interest their children to follow in their footsteps too. While half the kids running around the neighborhood may have dismissed their fathers as underachieving, middle-class "gofers," the other half want to be just like their dads. Have you ever noticed that businessmen seem to beget businesskids, preachers seem to produce midget ministers, educators seem to turn out teacher-tykes, and mechanics seem to make miniature Marios?

Their mantra is not "Be like Mike"; it's "Be like

Dad." (Can you say "Praise the Lord"?) What an awesome opportunity! What a tremendous challenge! What a great responsibility! Role-modeling.

When I was a little boy, I spent one rainy Saturday sitting in front of the hallway mirror, drawing self-portraits. First as a policeman, then as a doctor, and finally as a fireman. Looking back on it, I figure I was really into sirens for some reason. Perhaps I had just returned from one of my many trips to the emergency room of the local hospital, I don't know.

I do know that I was one of the most accident-prone kids in the neighborhood. My earliest recollection was of the afternoon I disobediently climbed the shelves in the garage to fetch a jar for the capture of a moth on the porch. I fell with the jar in my hand and was rushed to O'Conner Hospital for stitches.

Unfortunately for me, the poor sap on the other side of the curtain had just cut off his leg with a chainsaw, so my wound was pushed back on the triage. In an effort to hurry with me so they could get to him, instead of using anesthetic to ease my screaming pain, they simply poured water down my throat to choke me quiet. I must hand it to them—it was very effective.

That was followed by a broken collarbone sustained in a game of tackle football with a visiting behemoth three or four times my size. Then the skateboarding broken arm, the ant poison, the basketball broken arm, the metal ruler down my throat, the exploding ear, the tooth through the lip, the broken toes, the torn ligaments in ankles and knees. I'm a mess.

I eventually grew out of my attraction to emergency vehicles and, after seeing Willie Mays both in person and on television, I knew that I could one day play beside him. Or maybe even take his place in Candlestick's expansive centerfield. At that moment, baseball with the neighborhood wannabes became my personal pastime.

I didn't care that I didn't have the arm my brother seemed to have or the speed Ronnie ran with or the power Wes possessed. One over-the-shoulder catch convinced me that I would one day be in the record books, right alongside the "Say Hey" kid. His No. 24 right next to my No. 24½.

Obviously, that didn't happen. I barely made the high school varsity team in the one sport I could play, basketball, and except for a single shining moment or two on the college intramural team, my sports career has pretty much been relegated to my own driveway or backyard, where "my rules" allow me to reign undefeated.

For my sons, it was Mario Lemieux of the Pittsburgh Penguins, the graceful and powerful scorer of the NHL. For three years and hundreds of dollars worth of equipment and league fees, Ben the Bigger and Josh the Speedier mastered the ability to stay erect on in-line skates while passing and scoring seemingly at will. I was more than impressed . . . I was hopeful of huge, multiyear contracts.

But just as quickly and powerfully as it had come into our home, their interest in hockey faded. Once they traded in their sticks and pads for guitars and picks, their life's goal changed as well.

Eventually, of course, I became a teacher. Just like my dad. And my mom. And my sister. And my brother. But Dad was first, so I guess it was he who influenced the rest of us to follow that career path. And honestly, I can't think of a job I could love more (unless it would be David Letterman's).

When I was at the crossroads of choosing a career, I was mired in the curriculum of our church's seminary, not really wanting to be a pastor anymore. The girl I had planned to marry (she had been "called" to be a pastor's wife but couldn't even remain faithful to me in our engagement) was gone, and with her went my enthusiasm for the pulpit.

So one afternoon, as I sat on the couch I shared with five housemates, an acquaintance came over and began to focus in on my dilemma.

"Well, what do you want to be when you 'grow up'?" he asked, even though I was nearly 23 and he was maybe a year older.

"Oh, I don't know, Lonnie," I said.

"Hey, why don't you make a list of the three things you'd like to be, then. No regard to amount of preparation or costs or any other obstacle. Just dream. What would you like to be?" he asked a second time.

"OK," I said. "I want to be a rock-and-roll singer; I want to be a professional comedian; and I want to be the editor of a small-town weekly newspaper. That's what I want to be."

"So, go for it," he simply said. "Go for it."

What that did was free me up to think more broadly about ministry, a calling I sensed without reservation. "Yeah," I thought to myself, "I could serve God without writing weekly sermons or studying homiletics and hermeneutics, or philosophy or missions or church history. I might serve Him in a place and situation that would thrill me beyond my wildest dreams."

And that was the day I decided to leave my past burdens and transfer to the local university campus and pursue my first love—literature.

You know what? That list that I spilled out to Lonnie has come true too. Not only do I get to study and teach literature and writing, but I get to participate in our university's variety shows, where I have been both a "rock-and-roll star" and a "comedian." I have a captive audience two, three, four, sometimes even five hours a day, to practice my Steve Martin or Robin Williams or Dave Letterman routines. And as part of my job description, I am the faculty adviser for our weekly student newspaper, where I get to write and edit copy and help lead staff meetings.

As a professor, then, but mostly as a father, I have been able to find that God's will for our lives is not "Career Planning and Placement." Not at all. God's will for our lives is found at the end of Jesus' Great Sermon: chapter 7 of Matthew, verses 24-27.

"Therefore everyone who hears these words of mine and puts them into practice is like a wise man who built his house on the rock. The rain came down, the streams rose, and the winds blew and beat against that house; yet it did not fall, because it had its foundation on the rock. But everyone who hears these words of mine and does not put them into practice is like a foolish man who built his house on sand. The rain came down, the streams rose, and the winds blew and beat against that house, and it fell with a great crash."

God's "course of action" for His children is that they "build their houses on His foundation." On Him. Beautiful! How the children earn the money to buy the bricks and mortar for their houses is really up to them and their dreams. God instilled in us before we were born certain gifts, talents, and hopes. If we use them to build His kingdom, whatever they are—policeman, doctor, fireman, center fielder, preacher, teacher, rock-and-roll singer, comedian, editor—then we have found the center of His precious will for our lives.

And that's the single most important truth I have attempted to pass on to my two boys. Whatever they want to do for a life's career, I'm all for it. Whatever makes them happy. Whatever puts a smile on their faces as they get up and drive to work every day. As long as I don't have to buy any more hockey helmets or padded gloves.

And they build their homes on God's foundation.